ALSO BY LORETTA LAROCHE
Happy Talk

How Serious Is <u>This</u>?

How Serious Is This?

Seeing Humor in Daily Stress

by
Loretta LaRoche

Illustrated by Robin Ouellette

Lighthearted
Productions, Inc.
Plymouth, MA

Published by Lighthearted Productions, Inc.
15 Peter Road, Plymouth, MA 02360

For book trade ordering contact The Humor Potential, Inc.
15 Peter Road, Plymouth, MA 02360 tel. 1.508.224.2280

Printed by BookCrafters, Fredericksburg, VA

ISBN 0-9644014-8-7

Printed in the United States of America

Dedicated to
My mother
for her gift of laughter

Introduction

Over the years I have had the good fortune of meeting thousands of individuals from all over the world. It always amazes me how much we all have in common. When I look at what stresses us, we especially share the apparent need to overreact. We love to dramatize and escalate the simplest of situations. I often wonder what would happen if we all tape-recorded ourselves for one week and then played it back? Would we be shocked at the amount of negativity in our conversation? Would we be surprised at how often we turn the proverbial molehill into a mountain? Since this would be a time consuming project, why not begin by becoming more aware of how we become stressed?...

It is my hope that this little book of Wit and Wisdom will enable you to do that. The glasses can be the lens through which you see your stressors differently and help you gain new insight. I have used them myself in traffic and have received many a smile in return. The world needs more smiles and less conflict, let us begin with ourselves. When we lighten up, others will follow.

Joy, peace and laughter,

Loretta LaRoche

Loretta LaRoche

Contents

One

Stressed?
Let's Face It

"Castastrophizing and Awfulizing"

Stressed? Let's Face It

I firmly believe that a lot of stress can be handled with a big dose of common sense, lots of humor and a better grip on reality. We take life's little glitches and treat them as if they were as important as losing a job or as dangerous as being trapped in an avalanche. True, there are situations that are inconvenient, irritating or depressing, but a rational mind learns to discern the difference.

Too much "catastrophizing and awfulizing" can help trigger a response called "fight or flight". Walter B. Cannon, a physiologist at Harvard at the turn of the century, was the first to describe the "fight or flight" response as a series of biochemical changes that prepare you to deal with threats.

Primitive man needed quick bursts of energy to flee such predators as the Saber-toothed Tiger.

However, if you're in your car in a traffic jam and you're yelling at people who can't even hear you, you're mobilizing a response that is no longer useful. Since the body doesn't know whether it's in a cave or a car, it responds to what it *thinks* are your cries for help. Your pupils dilate to sharpen vision and your hearing becomes acute. Your heart rate, blood volume, and blood pressure go up. You start to perspire. Your hands and feet get cold, as blood is directed away from your extremities and digestive system into larger muscles that help you to fight or run. Your diaphragm and anus lock.(this could be where the real meaning of uptight comes from!) You reach for a spear. In front of you is a seventy-eight year old woman in a thirty-eight year old Buick. She's enjoying her day because she knows moments are precious. She doesn't realize that in back of her is a raving Neanderthal who perceives her to be a Behemoth!

How many times a day do you get ready to throw the spear? The threats can be real or imagined and can run the gamut from dealing with a Xerox machine that won't work, to a long line at the check-out counter; from a bad haircut to a misbehaving toddler. Virtually anything can trigger the response if you think or interpret the situation as harmful or threatening. Chronic "fight or flight" can seriously harm you both physically and emotionally. The bad news being that every body system can be damaged by stress. The good news is that we all have the ability to change our way of viewing life's events. We may not be able to change the situation, but we can see it differently.

The use of humor can be one of the greatest resources we have in helping us restore our perspective when we've become "hooked on catastrophizing". Dr. William Fry Jr., who has done extensive research documenting the physiological benefits of laughter, notes that fear and rage, two emotions associated with stress, are countered and alleviated by humor. "Humor acts to relieve fear", he states, "rage is impossible when mirth prevails".

Two

Grin And Bear It!

"How do you feel?"
"Fine."
"Then why don't you tell your face?"
Leo Buscaglia

Grin and Bear It!

"Put on a Happy Face", a songwriter once wrote. We may hum along, but that doesn't mean we buy into the program. Smiling like a campaigning politician (regardless of how you feel) seems insincere at best. Why force it?

One reason why, is that it actually might be good for you. Whereas smiles, frowns and grimaces once were seen as simple expressions of feeling, researchers are realizing that people's expressions play a physiological role in the regulation of their moods. Perhaps one of the most remarkable findings: facial expressions not only *reveal emotions*, they can *create them* as well. Manipulating the muscles and blood vessels of the face, it seems, may trigger chemical changes in the brain that make us measurably happier or sadder. The old cliche, *"Fake it 'til you make it"*, may indeed hold more truth then we ever imagined.

If this theory holds true, then a smile or wearing a pair of Groucho glasses could help us get through some of life's everyday struggles. In order to cope, we need to realize that being *stuck in traffic* and being *mugged* are not the same thing!

Three

From Misery to Mirth

Discovering the Humor in Life's Little Stressors

"If you don't have to suffer, don't practice!"
Loretta LaRoche

From Misery to Mirth

The following situations are typical stressors that people experience in everyday life. They are not earth shattering or life-threatening, however, when we add our own internal drama, they become more than we can handle. Learning to see the humor behind our own irrational thinking helps us to diffuse our stress and cope in a more functional manner. Wearing the Groucho glasses helps us to become more of a witness to our own behavior, which in turn gives us a better perspective. It may not be the total solution, but it is a beginning.

This is one way of *getting to the absurdity,* the integral part of shifting from *Misery to Mirth* and it can be done without the glasses as well. Once you find the humor, you will find yourself getting less upset. This, in turn, creates a calmer mind that can now focus its attention and energy towards solutions. Remember, you always have options.

My three favorites are:
* *Act* upon it,
* *Avoid* it, or
* *Accept* it!

The Grocery Store

Bored with food shopping? Sick of cashiers who can't find the code for lettuce? Tired of being in line with people who have fifty items in the express lane? And now they're going to pay with a check! Why do all these other people have to be here? Someone *else* is going to have to do our shopping from now on!

"Even if there's nothing to laugh at, laugh on credit!"
(anonymous)

Next time you go shopping, wear your glasses. Grab a cart and zoom around saying "BEEP... ..BEEP" just like the kids do. Not ready to go that far? Well, then just wear them when you pay for your groceries and ask the clerk to *"Check You Out!"*

Traffic

Stuck in traffic? Upset over drivers who probably failed Driver's Ed and landed in front of you? Disgusted because they decided to travel the same time you did and now you're late? You can feel your blood pressure rising, your shoulders tensing and you're gripping the wheel. You're starting to look like a dead parrot!

"The trouble with being in the rat race is, that even if you win, you're still a rat." Lily Tomlin

Put your glasses on and watch how others seem to let you merge right in! See the humor in every lane and when you get to your destination you'll be in a much better mood. Imagine how much you'll smile when you see yourself in the rearview mirror!

As you go through the toll booth

To the Registry of Motor Vehicles

The Weather

It's gray, cold, windy and they're predicting more snow. This is getting ridiculous. You've had enough. Everyday you're glued to the T.V. weather reports, waiting for a sign of warmth. Depression is setting in and you've decided that you'll stay inside until Spring!

"The most completely lost of all days, is the one in which we haven't laughed". *(French proverb)*

Get a grip! It's winter. Remember playing in the snow and wishing for a blizzard so school would close. Put on your glasses and go out and make a snow man. It *will* pass, get warm again, and the cycle will continue (unless you move to the Caribbean).

Waiting In Line

You've been waiting very, very patiently, but there are limits. Why is that person taking so long? Don't they realize there are other people in back of them? Oh No... they're taking a lunch break! Why do they have to eat on your time? This is it.. I'm going to hire someone to wait in line for me. Let them suffer!

"The journey of a thousand miles begins with the first step."
(Chinese proverb)

According to national statistics on standing in line, (yes, there was such a study) you will wait in line for three years of your life! Why not have fun during that time? When you feel yourself growing edgy, put on your glasses and whistle a happy tune. You might end up wishing the line was a little longer.

While waiting for your next flight

While shopping at the mall

The Dentist

You've put it off for months, but now it's just around the corner. How you've been dreading it... your mouth open 'til it hurts..the taste of rubber gloves...novocaine and of course THE DRILL! When will you ever hear *"You may rinse your mouth out... you're done!."*?

"Humor is the instinct for taking pain playfully."
Max Eastman

Imagine how you'd look without teeth! Not a good option. Go into the waiting room, sit down, put on your glasses, and start chatting with the other patients. Give your dentist a pair too! Then take a picture of the two of you to hang on your refrigerator. Look at it whenever you make a dental appointment.

The Doctor's Office

You had a three o'clock appointment and it's now midnight! Why do they book seventy people for the same time? And the magazines! If you read battered issues of "*Highlights for Children*" one more time, you're going to lose it completely! That's it, no more doctors for you, you're just going to stay home and suffer.

"There ain't much fun in medicine, but there's a whole lot of medicine in fun." Josh Billings

Bring your glasses to your next appointment. interview the other patients and ask them, *"What are <u>you</u> here for?"* It might bring a smile to their lips and to yours. It will definitely lighten up the waiting room and who knows, you might even get to see the doctor sooner than you thought.

When you take your child to the pediatrician

At the Gynecologist's Office

The Wedding

It's finally the day you've been waiting for. Months of planning. They are all seated waiting for you to take the big step. Your mind is playing Ping Pong. *"I can't wait"*, *"Oh No, what am I doing?"* Suddenly your heart is racing and you're getting a case of hives.

"The only thing you have to offer another human being, <u>ever</u>, is your state of being." Ram Dass

Do your whole wedding party and yourself a favor. Give them a pair of glasses. After you have exchanged your vows, turn and face the guests with your glasses on and walk back down the aisle. It will lighten everyone up.

Sex

You're tired. You've had a long day. You need to chill out and be alone, but he/she suggests a romantic interlude.
It's a dilemma, you want to fulfill your needs without guilt.

> *"Anything worth taking seriously is worth making fun of."*
> *Tom Lehrer*

Walk into the bedroom with your glasses on and tell him or her to start without you! Add, that when it sounds *good* ...you'll be in! Have some fun with an activity that is *supposed* to be fun. It may not solve the problem but it may add the element of delight.

Wear Your Glasses

On a Blind Date

When you're late for dinner

The In-Laws

They're coming for dinner for the first time. You're a wreck. They're probably going to notice the mismatched steak knives and the chipped china. They'll be listening to everything you say and analyzing it, so they can report you to the local newspaper. Why did you invite them? You must be a masochist!

"A laugh can be very powerful. In fact sometimes in life, it's the only weapon we have."   *Roger Rabbit*

Not to worry! Open the wine with great festivities. Put on your glasses, hand them each a pair and give a fabulous toast. As you sip your wine, tell them how lucky they are to have you in the family.

Parenting

Starting to wonder where these kids came from? Remember when your parents said "I hope you have children just like yourself!" Pretty scary, it's coming true! Just today you found soaking wet towels *on* the bed, the remains of a peanut butter sandwich *in* the bed and melted crayolas *under* the bed!

"It's never too late to have a happy childhood"
(anonymous)

When you're by yourself, put your glasses on, stand in front of the mirror and say all your thoughts out loud! By the time you're done you'll see things in a better light. Don't forget to *See* the humor in your family; it's the glue that will keep you together.

At the height of an argument with your teenager

Wear Your Glasses

When your toddler has a tantrum

Control Freak

You're totally scheduled for the next fifty years. Your time management is winning an Oscar this year. You get so much done that you're finished before you start! Why are there so many lazy, unorganized and irresponsible people in the world? Don't they get it? You're just going to have to start giving lectures to everyone and straighten them out!

"Life is not what it's supposed to be, it's the way it is."
Virginia Satir

Put your glasses on and announce to anyone who'll listen, that you are "The Director of the Universe." Have a party in your honor, invite all the people who can't get it together and tell them once and for all that you are the Control Czar.

Worrying

You're tossing and turning, desperately trying to get to sleep. It's impossible because you have so much on your mind. Bills, job insecurities, the kid's education, your weight, taxes.
How much can you stand? Will it ever end and now you can't sleep either!

"Nothing is good or bad, but thinking it makes it so."
Shakespeare

Make a pact with yourself to get up a half hour early, sit in a comfortable chair, get your coffee, put your glasses on and make a worry list. As you worry about each thing, check it off and go on to the next. When you go to bed at night, your worrying will have been done and you'll be free to sleep!

When you can't fall asleep

While you're paying your bills

Arguments

Why don't they just give up and say that you're right? After all, look at how many times you were! This has been going on for years. Look at all the evidence you brought up to support your side of the story! When are they going to admit that they *never* put the cap on the toothpaste?!

"We think very few people sensible except those that agree with us".
Francis De LaRochefoucauld

When things are getting close to volcanic, grab your glasses and yell "Time Out!". Go find a mirror, look at yourself and ask yourself this question "Do I want to be right, or do I want to be happy?" It just might put a little perspective on the matter.

Self Bashing

You've gained some weight, you got the wrong haircut again and your chin is reproducing itself. It's got to be all down hill from here. If only you hadn't eaten the whole pound cake. Maybe if you hadn't skipped aerobics! Maybe someone will Fedex you a new body!

"Tell me what you pay attention to and I will tell you who you are."
Jose Ortega Y Gasset

Time to appreciate who you are and the possibilities that are there. Stand in front of the mirror everyday with your glasses on and exclaim, *"I'm not too bad, and parts of me are even excellent!"*

Just before you make a speech

When trying on a bathing suit

Burnout

Sick and tired of being sick and tired? If only people would stop taking advantage of your competency, your generosity and your total goodness. *Someday* they'll know how much you've done for them...how much you've sacrificed! (And *that* will probably be after you've taken your last breath!)

"Human life is basically a comedy. Even its tragedies often seem comic to the spectator and not infrequently to the victim."
H.L.Menchen

Don't wait another minute! Put your glasses on, walk into your office or home and ask for a standing ovation! If no one pays attention to you, go next door and ask the neighbor to give you one.

The Diet

You're weighing everything you eat, you're counting grams of fat, your treadmill is your second home and still it's not coming off! How much is one person supposed to sacrifice? It's been like this for years... whatever you eat makes you fat! What's the use?

"Everything you see I owe to spaghetti"
Sophia Loren

Hang in there. It took time to accumulate, it takes time to reduce. Have fun with it. Wear your glasses to your next aerobic class and enjoy your new goals. Do it *Jest* for the health of it!

Wear Your Glasses

While you're taking your fitness walk

At your weekly "weigh-in"

Voice Mail

You press #1 because you have touchtone, then you press #3 to reach the right dept., you press #7 for customer service, somehow you're disconnected! You redial and now you're on hold and the music starts. If you wanted music you would have called Stevie Wonder! Whatever happened to real people answering the phone?

"Computers are useless. They can only give you answers."
Pablo Picasso

Relax! Put your glasses on and either sing along with the music or take some deep breaths. Eventually you'll get a human being. If that doesn't seem probable, leave a message and pray they'll call back, or try again later. In any case, it's not worth a heart attack.

The Office

Memos are coming in left and right. You're being faxed, E-mailed and paged! There are thirty-seven meetings scheduled for today. One of them is about re-engineering the company. There will be downsizing and cutbacks. You *know* you may be next! What will you do? You'll have no money, no food, no clothes. You'll be stark naked! What a mess!

"One of the symptoms of an approaching nervous breakdown is the belief that one's work is terribly important." Bertrand Russell

Yes, you *could* be part of the re-engineering plan or maybe not. Think of all the opportunities this could offer you and concentrate your energies on a *plan*, not a plot to make things worse. Put your glasses on, go find a mirror and say, "Oh Well, I can deal with it." It won't change things, but it may make them easier.

To staff meetings at work

When the copier breaks down

Perfectionism

You are so disgusted with the way people leave
things all over the place! Why can't they put
things back, like you do? And they borrow your
stuff and don't return it! Oh, and the way they
dress..totally mismatched. Not like you. You're
always color coordinated. You're sick to death of
it all. Why can't they be more like you?

"Perfection has one grave defect; it is apt to be dull."
W. Somerset Maugham

Chill out! People are different and they will continue to be that way unless you can figure out a way to clone yourself! Until that happens, put your glasses on and when someone is doing something *Their Way*, just look at them and say, "Isn't that interesting!".

Wear Your Glasses

While cleaning the house

Wear Your Glasses

While mowing the lawn

Being too Serious

There's just too much foolish behavior, too much laughter. After all, life is to be taken seriously. So many awful things are going on and you want to report them to as many people as you possibly can. Your parents told you to "wipe that stupid grin off your face" and that's what you did!

"What is a sense of humor?... a residing feeling of one's own absurdity. It is the ability to understand a joke and that the joke is oneself." Clifton Fadiman

Lighten Up! Misery is optional. Discover the "elf" in yourself. Go out into the universe and seek out joy and humor. It's there. Put on your glasses and try to be an optimist. Remember "Pessimists may be accurate, but they don't live as long!"

Smiling from Inside Out

1. When you wake up, put a smile on your face and announce, "I'm Back!"
2. Spend time with children. Four year olds in particular, supposedly they laugh at least four hundred times a day.
3. Increase your smile connections. Smile at more people during the day... it will come back to you.
4. Consider spending part of each day smiling about what you *have* instead of what you *need*.
5. When you smile at someone, look into their eyes... it is the gateway to their soul.

Reading List

Benson, Herbert M.D. & Eileen Stuart, R.N., M.S.
 The Wellness Book: Carol Publishing; NY 1992
Borysenko, Joan Ph.D. & Miroslav Borysenko, Ph.D.
 The Power of the Mind to Heal: Hay House; CA 1994
Cousins, Norman
 Head First, The Biology of Hope: Harper & Row; NY 1989
Klein, Allen
 Humor and Healing: Jeremy Tarcher; CA 1989
Matthews, Andrew
 Being Happy!: Price Stern Sloan; CA 1988

Myers, David G., Ph.D.

The Pursuit of Happiness: William Morrow & Co.; NY 1992

Schuller, Robert H.

The Be Happy Attitudes: Bantam Books; NY 1987

Seigel, Bernie M.D.

Peace, Love and Healing: Harper & Row; NY 1988

Seligman, Martin E.P., Ph. D.

Learned Optimism: Alfred A. Knopf; NY 1992

True, Herb & Anna Mang

Humor Power: How to Get It, Give It and Gain:
Doubleday & Company, Inc.; NY 1980

Dear Reader:

We would love to hear about any steps you might be taking to see more humor in your life. We also welcome your humorous stories and/or photos utilizing the Groucho Glasses.

Please Send to:

Loretta LaRoche
c/o The Humor Potential
15 Peter Road
Plymouth, MA 02360

Loretta LaRoche is an educator, humorist and motivational speaker. She lectures nationally and internationally on various topics including:

"How to Prevent Hardening of the Attitude"
(Managing Stress Through Humor and Choice)

"Love, Laughter and Lasagna"
"Surviving Change Through Wit and Wisdom"
" Whine, Women and Song"
and "Parenting with Humor".

For Information on Loretta's Seminars and catalog call:
1-508-224-2280

Notes

(Use these pages for writing down situations where you could use "the glasses", for inserting your Groucho photos, or just for doodling!)